ONWARD AND PUPWARD!

A PAW Patrol Guide to Everything That Flies!

Pup, pup and away!

These pups gotta fly!

Join the PAW Patrol as they explore amazing aircraft from hang gliders to hoverboards, and helicopters to hot air balloons!

Airplanes

An airplane is a large flying vehicle with wings and propellers. Planes are used for transportation, sight-seeing and rescue missions! Some people even learn to fly small planes as a hobby.

DID YOU KNOW?

Someone who flies an aircraft is called a pilot.

Robo-Dog is the pilot of the PAW Patrol's awesome plane, The Air Patroller!

Seaplanes

Seaplanes are airplanes that can float like boats! That means they can take off from and land on water. These planes are mostly used for traveling to small islands, between lakes, or in remote areas.

Ready, set, get wet!

DID YOU KNOW?

From 1927 to 1939, seaplanes were the fastest aircrafts in the world!

Fighter Jets

Fighter jets are special airplanes mostly used by the military. They're also common at airshows because pilots can do amazing tricks with them! They fly upside down, make tight turns, do barrel rolls, and more!

They're heroes of the sky!

Helicopters

Helicopters are very agile—that means they can move quickly and easily! A helicopter has propellers that let it take off and land without a runway, which makes them great for landing in tight spots.

Time to fly!

DID YOU KNOW?

Helicopters can hover in one spot and fly backward!

DID YOU KNOW?

A hot air balloon's pilot can control how high up the balloon goes by opening a vent in the top of the balloon.

Hot Air Balloons

Hot air balloons were the first vehicles to carry people into the air. They work by heating up the air inside a big balloon. The hot air causes the balloon to lift a basket full of passengers up into the sky! These days, people ride in hot air balloons for sightseeing excursions and adventure.

Ready for takeoff!

Blimps

Blimps can fly because they're filled with helium, a gas that's lighter than air. Because they don't need to use any energy to stay afloat, they can remain in the air for hours or even days. This makes blimps great for things like covering sports events or even some scientific research, like scouting for whales!

You can steer a blimp with a rudder— just like on a boat!

DID YOU KNOW? Helium is the same gas that makes birthday balloons float!

DID YOU KNOW?

Stunt kites have two strings so they can do amazing tricks in the air, like flips and spins!

Kites

People have been making kites for more than 2,000 years! In the past, kites were used as signals or for scientific experiments like checking the temperature of the air. Today, people mostly fly kites for entertainment or in competitions!

Let's go fly a kite!

Paper Airplanes

A paper airplane can be made anywhere—you just need to fold a piece of paper the right way, like this:

1.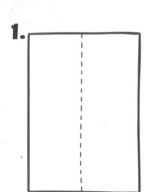

2.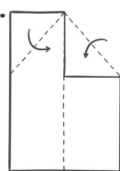

3.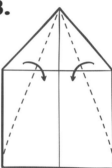

4.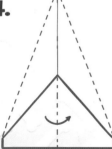

5.

6.

Making paper airplanes can be a great way to recycle paper!

DID YOU KNOW?

The farthest anyone has ever flown a hang glider is 475 miles. The pilot crossed most of Texas in 11 hours!

Hang Gliders

Hang gliders are non-motorized aircrafts that fly by only using wind power. The pilot launches the hang glider by running downhill into the wind! People like to ride in hang gliders as a sport and to see amazing sights.

What a PAWfect pilot!

Hoverboards

Hoverboards are a very new invention that engineers are still working on! They can only hold one person—or pup!—at a time. Some hoverboards can stay in the air for up to 10 minutes and have a top speed of more than 90 miles per hour—that's faster than a car on a highway!

Let's shred some clouds!

DID YOU KNOW?
To "hover" means to stay in the air without falling!

DID YOU KNOW?

Rockets were originally used for fireworks and for rescuing people at sea!

Rockets

Rockets are flying vehicles that can travel all the way to outer space! In order to go that far, rockets need to burn a lot of fuel. Burning the fuel causes gases to shoot out the bottom, and that pushes the rocket into the sky!

Let's take to outer space!

Drones

Drones are a lot like remote-controlled planes, except they can usually go a lot farther and can be controlled more easily. People use drones for all sorts of things—racing, taking pictures, looking for missing people, making deliveries, or even just for fun!

Fly high, dream big!

DID YOU KNOW?

A drone's wingspan can be smaller than a few inches or more than 100 feet!

DID YOU KNOW?

For now, jet packs aren't a very useful way to get around on Earth, but astronauts use them in outer space!

Jet Packs

Jet packs are devices people wear on their backs or strap to their feet that push out a lot of gas or water, and that makes a person fly! Jet packs can't travel very far—the record is 26 miles, and it took almost five hours! A car could make that trip in 30 minutes.

Time for lift off!

Dream Big, Fly High!

Media Lab Books
For inquiries, call 646-838-6637

Copyright 2017 Topix Media Lab

Published by Topix Media Lab
14 Wall Street, Suite 4B
New York, NY 10005

Printed in China

ISBN-10: 1-942556-96-9
ISBN-13: 978-1-942556-96-1